Prophet Isa (Jesus)

and

Maryam Bint Imran

(Virgin Mary)

English Edition

by

Jannah Firdaus Mediapro

2019

The Life of Prophet Isa AS (Jesus) & Maryam Bint Imran (Virgin Mary) English Edition

Copyright © 2019

Jannah Firdaus Mediapro

All rights reserved.

Prolog

In many verses of the Glorious Qur'an Allah SWT (God) The Exalted denied the claim of the Christians that He has a son. A delegation from Nagran came to the Prophet Muhammad SAW. They began to talk about their claim about the Trinity, which is that Allah is three in one, the Father, the Son, and the Holy Spirit, with some disagreement among their sects.

That is why Allah SWT (God) affirmed in many verses of The Noble Qur'an that Prophet Isa AS (Jesus) is a slave of Allah, whom He molded in the womb of his mother like any other of His creatures, and that He created him without a father, as He created Prophet Adam AS without a father or a mother.

The Life of Prophet Isa AS (Jesus) & Maryam (Virgin Mary)

Allah the Almighty said: *Allah chose Adam, Noah, the family of Abraham and the family of Imran above the Alamin (mankind and jinns)(of their times). Offspring, one of theo other, and Allah is All-Hearer, All-Knower.*

Remember when the wife of Imran said: "O my Lord! I have vowed to You what (the child that) is in my womb to be dedicated for Your services (free from all worldly work; to serve Your Place of worship), so accept this, from me. Verily, You are the All-Hearer, the All Knowing."

Then when she delivered her (child Mary), she said: "O my Lord! I have delivered a female child," and Allah knew better what she delivered, - "and the male is not like the female, and I have named her Mary, and I seek refuge with You (Allah) for her and for her offspring from Satan, the outcast."

So her Lord (Allah) accepted her with goodly acceptance. He made her grow in a good manner and put her under the care of Zechariah. Every time he entered Al-Mihrab (a praying place or a private room), he found her supplied with sustenance.

He said: "O Mary! From where have you got this?"

She said: "From Allah. Verily, Allah provides sustenance to whom He wills, without limit." (Ch 3:33-37 Quran)

Allah declared that He had elected Adam (pbuh) and the elite of his offspring who obey Allah. Then He specified the family of Abraham (pbuh), which includes the sons of Ishmael (pbuh), and the family of Imran, the father of Mary.

Muhammad Ibn Ishaaq stated that he was Imran Ibn Bashim, Ibn Amun, Ibn Misha, Ibn Hosqia, Ibn Ahriq, Ibn Mutham, Ibn Azazia, Ibn Amisa, Ibn Yamish, Ibn Ahrihu, Ibn Yazem, Ibn Yahfashat, Ibn Eisha, Ibn Iyam, Ibn Rahba am, Ibn David (Dawud).

Prophet Zakariyah's (pbuh) wife's sister had a daughter named Hannah. She was married to Imran, a leader of the Israelites. For many years, the couple remained childless. Whenever Hannah saw another woman with a child, her longing for a baby increased. Although years had passed, she never lost hope. She believed that one day Allah would bless her with a child, on whom she would shower all her motherly love.

She turned to the Lord of the heavens and the earth and pleaded with Him for a child. She would offer the child in the service of Allah's house, in the temple of Jerusalem. Allah granted her request. When she learned that she was pregnant, she was the happiest woman alive, and thanked Allah for His gift. Her overjoyed husband Imran also thanked Allah for His mercy.

However, while she was pregnant her husband passed away. Hannah wept bitterly. Alas, Imran did not live to see their child for whom they had so longed. She gave birth to a girl, and again turned to Allah in prayer: *"O my Lord, I have delivered a female child," and the male is not like the female, and I have named her Mary, and I seek refuge with You (Allah) for her and her offspring from Satan, the outcast." (Ch 3:36 Quran)*

Hannah had a big problem in reference to her promise to Allah, for females were not accepted into the temple, and she was very worried. Her sister's husband Zakariyah, comforted her, saying that Allah knew best what she had delivered and appreciated fully what she had offered in His service. She wrapped the baby in a shawl and handed it over to the temple elders. As the baby was a girl, the question of her guardianship posed a problem for the elders. This was a child of their late and beloved leader, and everyone was eager to take care of her. Zakariyah said to the elders: "I am the husband of her maternal aunt and her nearest relation in the temple; therefore, I will be more mindful of her than all of you."

As it was their custom to draw lots to solve disagreements, they followed this course. Each one was given a reed to throw into the river. They had agreed that whoever's reed remained afloat would be granted guardianship of the girl. All the reeds sank to the bottom except Zakariyah's. With this sign, they all surrendered to the will of Allah and made him the guardian.

To ensure that no one had access to Mary, Zakariyah built a separate room for her in the temple. As she grew up, she spent her time in devotion to Allah. Zakariyah visited her daily to see to her needs, and so it continued for many years. One day, he was surprised to find fresh fruit, which was out of season in her room. As he was the only person who could enter her room, he asked her how the fruit got there. She replied that these provisions were from Allah, as He gives to whom He wills. Zakariyah understood by this that Allah had raised Mary's status above that of other women.

Thereafter, Zakariyah spent more time with her, teaching and guiding her. Mary grew to be a devotee of Allah, glorifying Him day and night.

Ali Ibn Abi Talib narrated that the Prophet Muhammad (pbuh) said: "The best of the world's women is Mary (in her lifetime), and the best of the world's women is Khadija (in her lifetime)." (Sahih Al-Bukhari)

Abu Musa Al-Ashari also narrated that the Prophet Muhammad (pbuh) said: "May among men attained perfection but among women none attained perfection except Mary the daughter of Imran, and Asiya the wife of Pharaoh, and the superiority of Aisha to other women is like the superiority of Tharid (an Arabic dish) to other meals."

While Mary was praying in her temple, an angel in the form of a man appeared before her. Filled with terror, she tried to flee, praying: *"Verily! I seek refuge with the Most Beneficent (Allah) from you, if you do fear Allah."*

The angel said: "I am only a Messenger from your Lord, (to announce) to you the gift of a righteous son."

She said: "How can I have a son, when no man has touched me, nor am I unchaste?"

He said: "So (it will be), your Lord said: "That is easy for me (Allah): And (We wish) to appoint him as a sign to mankind and a mercy from Us (Allah), and it is a matter (already) decreed, (by Allah).'" (Ch 19:18-21 Quran)

The angel's visit caused Mary great anxiety, which increased as the months went by. How could she face giving birth to a child without having a husband? Later, she felt life kicking inside her. With a heavy heart, she left the temple and went to Nazareth, the city in which she had been born where she settled in a simple farm house to avoid the public.

But fear and anxiety did not leave her. She was from a noble and pious family. Her father had not been an evil man nor was her mother an impure woman. How could she prevent tongues from wagging about her honor?

After some months, she could not bear the mental strain any longer. Burdened with a heavy womb, she left Nazareth, not knowing where to go to be away from this depressing atmosphere.

She had not gone far, when she was overtaken by the pains of childbirth. She saw down against a dry palm tree, and here she gave birth to a son. Looking at her beautiful baby, she was hurt that she had brought him into the world without a father. She exclaimed: "I wish I had died before this happened and had vanished into nothingness!"

Suddenly, she heard a voice nearby: "Grieve not, your Lord has placed a rivulet below, and shake the trunk of this tree, from which ripe dates will fall. So eat and drink and regain the strength you have lost; and be of good cheer, for what you see is the power of Allah, Who made the dry palm tree regain life, in order to provide food for you." For a while she was comforted by Allah's miracle, for it was a sure sign of her innocence and purity.

She decided to return to the city. However, her fears also returned. What was she going to tell the people? As if sharinhis mother's worry, the baby began to speak: "If you meet any person say: 'I have vowed to fast for The Beneficent and may not speak to any human today.'" With this miracle, Mary felt at ease.

As she had expected, her arrival in the city with a newborn baby in her arms aroused the curiosity of the people. They scolded her: "This is a terrible sin that you have committed." She put her finger to her lips and pointed to the child. They asked: "How can we speak to a newborn baby?" To their total amazement, the child began to speak clearly: "I am Allah's servant. Allah has given me the Book, and has made me a prophet, and has blessed me wherever I may be, and has enjoined on me prayers and alms-giving as long as I live. Allah has made me dutiful towards she who had borne me. He has not made me arrogant nor unblessed. Peace unto me the day I was born, the day I die, and the day I shall be raised alive."

Most of the people realized that the baby was unique, for it Allah wills something, He merely says "Be" and it happens. Of course, there were some who regarded the baby's speech as a strange trick, but at least Mary could now stay in Nazareth without being harassed.

Allah the Exalted revealed: *And mention in the Book (the Qur'an, O Muhammad, the story of) Mary, when she withdrew in seclusion from her family to a place facing east. She placed a screen (to screen herself) from them; then We sent to her Our Ruh (angel Gabriel), and he appeared before her in the form of a man in all respects.*

She said: "Verily! I seek refuge with the Most Beneficent (Allah) from you, if you do fear Allah."

The angel said: "I am only a Messenger from your Lord, (to announce) to you the gift of a righteous son."

She said: "How can I have a son, when no man has touched me, nor am I unchaste?" He said: "So (it will be), your Lord said: "That is easy for Me (Allah): and (We wish) to appoint him as a sign to mankind and a mercy from Us (Allah), and it is a matter (already) decreed, (by Allah).'"

So she conceived him, and she withdrew with him to a far place (Bethlehem valley, about four to six miles from Jerusalem). And the pains of childbirth drove her to the trunk of a palm tree. She said: "Would that I had died before this, and had been forgotten and out of sight!"

Then (the babe "Jesus" or Gabriel) cried unto her from below her, saying: "Grieve not! Your Lord has provided you a water stream under you; and shake the trunk of palm tree towards you, it will let fall fresh ripe dates upon you. So eat and drink and be glad, and if you see any human being, say: 'Verily! I have vowed a fast unto the Most Beneficent (Allah) so I shall not speak to any human being this day.'"

Then she brought him (the baby) to her people, carrying him. They said: "O Mary! Indeed you have brought a thing Fariyya (an unheard mighty thing). O sister (the like) of Aaron (not the brother of Moses, but he was another pious man at the time of Mary)! Your father was not a man who used to commit adultery, nor was your mother an unchaste woman."

Then she pointed to him. They said: "How can we talk to one who is a child in the cradle?"

He (Jesus) said: "Verily! I am a slave of Allah. He has given me the Scripture and made me a Prophet; and He has made me blessed wheresoever I be, and has enjoined me prayer, and Zakat, as long as I live, and dutiful to my mother, and made me not arrogant, unblest. And Salam (peace) be upon me the day I was born, and the day I die, and the day I shall be raised alive!"

Such is Jesus, son of Mary. (It is) a statement of truth, about which they doubt (or dispute). It befits not (the Majesty of) Allah that He should beget a son (this refers to the slander of Christians against Allah, by saying that Jesus is the son of Allah). Glorified (and Exalted be He above all that they associate with Him). When He decrees a thing, He only says to it, "Be!" - and it is.

Jesus said: "And verily Allah is my Lord and your Lord. So worship Him (Alone). That is the Straight Path. (Allah's Religion of Islamic Monotheism which He did ordain for all of His Prophets)."

Then the sects differed (the Christians about Jesus), so woe unto the disbeliveers (those who gave false witness saying that Jesus is the son of Allah) from the meeting of a great Day (the Day of Resurrection, when they will be thrown in the blazing Fire).

How clearly will they (polytheists and disbeliveers in the Oneness of Allah) see and hear, the Day when they will appear before Us! But the Zalimun (polytheists and wrong-doers) today are in plain error. And warn them (O Muhammad) of the Day of grief and regrets, when the case has been decided, while now they are in a state of carelessness and they believe not. (Ch 19:16-39 Quran)

It was said that Joseph the Carpenter was greatly surprised when he knew the story, so he asked Mary: "Can a tree come to grow without a seed?" She said: "Yes, the one which Allah created for the first time."

He asked her again: "Is it possible to bear a child without a male partner?" She said: "Yes, Allah, created Adam without male or female!"

It was also said that, while pregnant, Mary went one day to her aunt, who reported that she felt as if she was pregnant. Mary in turn, said that she, too, was feeling as if she was pregnant. Then her aunt said: "I can see what is in my womb prostrating to what is in your womb."

The Jewish priests felt this child Jesus was dangerous, for they felt that the people would turn their worship to Allah the Almighty Alone, displacing the existing Jewish tenets. Consequently, they would lose their authority over the people. Therefore, they kept the miracle of Jesus's speech in infancy as a secret and accused Mary of a great misdeed.

As Jesus (pbuh) grew, the signs of prophethood began to increase. He could tell his friends what kind of supper waited for them at home and what they had hidden and where. When he was twelve years old, he accompanied his mother to Jerusalem. There he wandered into the temple and joined a crowd listening to the lecture of the Rabbis (Jewish priests). The audience were all adults, but he was not afraid to sit with them. After listening intently, he asked questions and expressed his opinion. The learned rabbis were disturbed by the boy's boldness and puzzled by the questions he asked, for they were unable to answer him. They tried to silence him, but he ignored their attempts and continued to express his views. Jesus became so involved in this exchange that he forgot he as expected back home.

In the meantime, his mother went home, thinking that he might have gone back with relatives or friends. When she arrived, she discovered that he was not there, so she returned to the city to look for him. At last she found him in the temple, sitting among the learned, conversing with them. He appeared to be quite at east, as if he had been doing this all his life. Mary got angry with him for causing her worry. He tried to assure her that all the arguing and debating with the learned had made him forgot the time.

Jesus grew up to manhood. It was Sabbath, a day of complete rest: no fire could be lit or extinguished nor could females plait their hair. Moses (pbuh) had commanded that Saturday be dedicated to the worship of Allah. However, the wisdom behind the Sabbath and its spirit had gone, and only the letter remained in the Jews' hearts. Also, they thought that Sabbath was kept in heaven, and that the People of Israel had been chosen by Allah only to observe the Sabbath.

They made a hundred things unlawful on Saturday even self-defense or calling a doctor to save a patient who was in bad condition. This is how their life was branded by such hypocrisy. Although the Pharisees were guardians of the law, they were ready to sell it when their interests were involved so as to obtain personal gains. There was, for example, a rule which prohibited a journey of more than one thousand yards on the Sabbath day. What do we expect of the Pharisees in this case? The day before, they transferred their food and drink from their homes two thousand yards away and erected a temporary house so that from tthey could travel a further thousand yards on the Sabbath day.

Jesus was on his way to the temple. Although it was the Sabbath, he reached out his hand to pick two pieces of fruit to feed a hungry child. This was considered to be a violation of the Sabbath law. He made a fire for the old women to keep themselves warm from the freezing air. Another violation. He went to the temple and looked around. There were twenty thousand Jewish priests registered there who earned their living from the temple. The rooms of he temple were full of them.

Jesus observed that the visitors were much fewer than the priests. Yet the temple was full of sheep and doves which were sold to the people to be offered as sacrifices. Every step in the temple cost the visitor money. They worshipped nothing but money. In the temple, the Pharisees and Sadducees acted as if it were a market place, and these two groups always disagreed on everything. Jesus followed the scene with his eyes and observed that the poor people who could not afford the price of the sheep or dove were swept away like flies by the Pharisees and Saducees. Jesus was astonished. Why did the priests burn a lot of offerings inside the temple, while thousands of poor people were hungry outside it?

On this blessed night, the two noble prophets John (pbuh) and Zakariyah (pbuh) died, killed by the ruling authority. On the same night, the revelation descended upon Jesus (pbuh). Allah the Exalted commanded him to begin his call to the children of Israel. To Jesus, the life of ease was closed, and the page of worship and struggled was opened.

Like an opposing force, the message of Jesus came to denounce the practices of the Pharisees and to reinforce the Law of Moses. In the face of a materialistic age of luxury and worship of gold, Jesus called his people to a nobler life by word and deed. This exemplary life was the only way out of the wretchedness and diseases of his age. Jesus's call, from the beginning, was marked by its complete uprightness and piety. It appealed to the soul, the inner being, and not be a closed system of rules laid down by society.

Jesus continued inviting the people to Almighty Allah. His call was based on the principle that there is no mediation between the Creator and His creatures. However, Jesus was in conflict with the Jews' superficial interpretation of the Torah. He said that he did not come to abrogate the Torah, but to complete it by going to the spirit of its substance to arrive at its essence.

He made the Jews understand that the Ten Commandments have more value than they imagined.

For instance, the fifth commandment does not only prohibit physical killing, but all forms of killing; physical, psychological, or spiritual. And the sixth commandment does not prohibit adultery only in the sense of unlawful physical contact between a man and a woman, but also prohibits all forms of unlawful relations or acts that might lead to adultery. The eye commits adultery when it looks at anything with passion.

Jesus was therefore in confrontation with the materialistic people. He told them to desist from hypocrisy, show and false praise. There was no need to hoard wealth in this life. They should not preoccupy themselves with the goods of this passing world; rather they must preoccupy themselves with the affairs of the coming world because it would be everlasting.

Jesus told them that caring for this world is a sin, not fit for pious worshippers. The disbeliveers care for it because they do not know a better way. As for the believers, they know that their sustenance is with Allah, so they trust in Him and scorn this world.

Jesus continued to invite people to worship the Only Lord, Who is without partner, just as he invited them to purify the heart and soul.

His teaching annoyed the priests, for every word of Jesus was a threat to them and their position, exposing their misdeeds.

The Roman occupiers had, at first, no intention of being involved in this religious discord of the Jews because it was an internal affair, and they saw that this dispute would distract the Jews from the question of the occupation.

However, the priests started to plot against Jesus. They wanted to embarrass him and to prove that he had come to destroy the Mosaic Law. The Mosaic Law provides that an adulteress be stoned to death. They brought him a Jewish adulteress and asked Jesus: "Does not the law stipulate the stoning of the adulteress?" Jesus answered: "Yes." They said: "This woman is an adulteress." Jesus looked at the woman and then at the priests. He knew that they were more sinful than she. They agreed that she should be killed according to Mosaic Law, and they understood that if he was going to apply Mosaic Law, he would be destroying his own rules of forgiveness and mercy.

Jesus understood their plan. He smiled and assented: "Whoever among you is sinless can stone her." His voice rose in the middle of the Temple, making a new law on adultery, for the sinless to judge sin. There was none eligible; no mortal can judge sin, only Allah the Most Merciful.

As Jesus left the temple, the woman followed him. She took out a bottle of perfume from her garments, knelt before his feet and washed them with perfume and tears, and then dried his feet with her hair. Jesus turned to the woman and told her to stand up, adding: "O

Lord, forgive her sins." He let the priests understand that those who call people to Almighty Allah are not executioners. His call was based on mercy for the people, the aim of all divine calls.

Jesus continued to pray to Allah for mercy on his people and to teach his people to have mercy on one another and to believe in Allah.

Jesus continued his mission, aided by divine miracles. Some Qur'anic commentators said that Jesus brought four people back from the dead: a friend of his named Al-Azam, an old woman's son, and a woman's only daughter. These three had died during his lifetime. When the Jews saw this they said: "You only resurrect those who have died recently; perhaps they only fainted." They asked him to bring back to life Sam the Ibn Noah.

When he asked them to show him his grave, the people accompanied him there. Jesus invoked Allah the Exalted to bring him back to life and behold, Sam the Ibn Noah came out from the grave gray-haired. Jesus asked: "how did you get gray hair, when there was no aging in your time?" He answered: "O Spirit of Allah, I thought that the Day of Resurrection had come; from the fear of that day my hair turned gray."

Allah the Almighty said: *Remember when Allah will say (on the Day of Resurrection): "O Jesus, son of Mary! Remember My Favor to you and to your mother when I supported you with Ruh-ul-Qudus (Gabriel) so that you spoke to the people in the cradle and in maturity; and when I taught you writing, Al Hikmah (the power of understanding), the Torah and the Gospel; and when you made out of the clay, as it were, the figure of a bird, by My Permission, and you breathed into it, and it became a bird by My Permission, and you healed those born blind, and the lepers by My Permission, and when you brought forth the dead by My Permission; and when I restrained the Children of Israel from you (when they resolved to kill you) since you came unto them with clear proofs, and the disbeliveers among them said: 'This is nothing but evident magic.'"*

And when I (Allah) put in their hearts of the disciples (of Jesus) to believe in Me and My Messenger, they said: "We believe. And bear witness that we are Muslims." (Ch 5:110-111 Quran)

Almighty Allah also revealed: And He Allah will teach him (Jesus) the Book and Al Hikmah (the Sunna, the faultless speech of the Prophets, wisdom, etc.), (and) the Torah and the Gospel.

And will make him (Jesus) a Messenger to the Children of Israel (saying): "I have come to you with a sign from your Lord, that I design for you out of clay, as it were, the figure of a bird, and breathe into it, and it becomes a bird by Allah's Leave; and I heal him who was born blind, and the leper, and I bring the dead to life by Allah's leave. And I inform you of what you eat, and what you store in your houses. Surely, therein is a sign for you, if you believe. And I have come confirming that which was before me of the Torah, and to make lawful to you part of what was forbidden to you, and I have come to you with proof from your Lord. So fear Allah and obey me. Truly! Allah is my Lord and your Lord, so worship Him (Alone). This is the Straight Path."

Then when Jesus came to know of their disbelief, he said: "Who will be my helpers in Allah's Cause?" The disciples said: "We are the helpers of Allah; we believe in Allah, and bear witness that we are Muslims (we submit to Allah)."

Our Lord! We believe in what You have sent down, and we follow the Messenger (Jesus); so write us down among those who bear witness (to the truth, La ilaha ill Allah - none has the right to be worshipped but Allah).

And they (disbeliveers) plotted (to kill Jesus), and Allah planned too. And Allah is the Best of the planners. (Ch 3:48-54 Quran)

Jesus continued calling people to Almighty Allah and laying down for them what might be called "the law of the Spirit." Once when standing on a mountain surrounded by his disciples, Jesus saw that those who believed in him were from among the poor, the wretched, an the downtrodden, and their number was small. Some of the miracles which Jesus performed had been requested by his disciples, such as their wish for a "holy table" to be sent down from heaven.

Allah the Exalted said: *Remember when the disciples said: "O Jesus, son of Mary! Can your Lord send down to us a table spread (with food) from heaven?" Jesus said: "Fear Allah, if you are indeed believers." They said: "We wish to eat thereof and to be stronger in Faith and to know that you have indeed told us the truth and that we ourselves be its witnesses."*

Jesus, son of Mary, said: "O Allah, our Lord! Send us from heaven a table spread (with food) that there may be for us - for the first and the last of us - a festival and a sign from You; and provide us sustenance, for You are the best of sustainers." Allah said: "I am going to send it down unto you, but if any of you after that disbelieves, then I will punish him with a torment such as I have not inflicted on anyone among all the Alamin (mankind and jinn)." (Ch 5:112-115 Quran)

It was related that Jesus commanded his disciples to fast for thirty days; at the end of it, they asked Jesus to bring food from heaven to break their fast. Jesus prayed to Allah after his disciples had doubted Allah's power. The great table cam down between two clouds, one above and one below, while the people watched. Jesus said: "O Lord, make it a mercy and not a cause of distress." So it fell between Jesus's hands, covered with a napkin.

Jesus suddenly prostrated and his disciples with him. They sensed a fragrance, which they had never smelled before. Jesus said: "The one who is the most devout and most righteous may uncover the table, that we might eat of it to thank Allah for it." They said: "O Spirit of Allah, you are the most deserving."

Jesus stood up, then performed ablution and prayed before uncovering the table, and behold, there was a roasted fish. The disciples said: "O Spirit of Allah, is this the food of this world or of Paradise?" Jesus said to his disciples: "Did not Allah forbid you to ask questions? It is the divine power of Allah the Almighty Who said: 'Be,' and it was. It is a sign from Almighty Allah warning of great punishment for unbelieving mortals of the world. This is the kernel of the matter."

It is said that thousands of people partook of it, and yet they never exhausted it. A further miracle was that the blind and lepers were cured.

The Day of the Table became one of the holy days for the disciples and followers of Jesus. Later on, the disciples and followers forgot the real essence of the miracles, and so they worshipped Jesus as a god.

Almighty Allah asserted: *And remember when Allah will say (on the Day of Resurrection): "O Jesus, son of Mary! Did you say unto men: 'Worship me and my mother as two gods besides Allah?'" He will say: "Glory be to You! It was not for me to say what I had no right to say. Had I said such a thing, You would surely have known it. You know what is in my inner self though I do not know what is in Yours, truly, You, only You, are the All Knower of all that is hidden and unseen. Never did I say to them aught except what You (Allah) did command me to say: 'Worship Allah, my*

Lord and your Lord', And I was a witness over them while I dwelt amongst them, but when You took me up, You were the Watcher over them, and You are a Witness to all things. (This is a great admonition and warning to the Christians of the whole world). If you punish them, they are Your slaves, and if You forgive them, Verily You, only You are the All Mighty, the All Wise."

Allah will say: "This is a Day on which the truthful will profit from their truth: theirs are Gardens under which rivers flow (in Paradise) - they shall abide therein forever. Allah is pleased with them and they with Him. That is the great success (Paradise). To Allah belongs the dominion of the heavens and the earth and all that is therein, and He is Able to do all things." (Ch 5:116-120 Quran)

Jesus went on his mission until vice knew that its throne was threatening to fall. So the forces of evil accused him of magic, infringement of the Mosaic Law, allegiance with the devil; and when they saw that the poor people followed him, they began to scheme against him.

The Sanhedrin, the highest judicial and ecclesiastical council of the Jews, began to meet to plot against Jesus. The plan took a new turn. When the Jews failed to stop Jesus' s call, they decided to kill him. The chief priests held secret meetings to agree on the best way of getting rid of Jesus. While they were in such a meeting, one of the twelve apostles of Jesus, Judas Iscariot, went to them and asked: "What will you give me if I deliver him to you?" Judas bargained with them until they agreed to give him thirty pieces of silver known as shekels. The plot was laid for the capture and murder of Jesus.

It was said that the high priest of the Jews tore his garment at the meeting, claiming that Jesus had denied Judaism. The tearing of clothes at that time was a sign of disgust.

The priests had no authority to pass the death sentence at that time, so they convinced the Roman governor that Jesus was plotting against the security of the Roman Empire and urged him to take immediate action against him. The governor ordered thaJesus be arrested.

According to the Book of Matthew, Jesus was arrested and the council of the high priests passed the death sentence upon him. Then, they began insulting him, spitting on his face and kicking him.

It was the Roman custom for the condemned to be flogged before they were executed. So Pilate, the Roman governor, ordered that Jesus be flogged. The Mosaic Law stipulates forty lashes, but the Roman had no limit, and they were brutal lashes. After that, Jesus was handed to the soldiers for crucifixion. They took off his clothes, and kept them. They put a crown of thorns on his head to mock him. According to custom he carried his cross on his back to increase his suffering.

Finally, they reached a place called Golgotha, meaning the Place of Skulls, outside the walls of Jerusalem. Instead of giving him a cup of wine diluted with scent to help lessen the pain on the cross, the soldiers gave Jesus a cup of vinegar diluted with gall. Then they crucified him and, as a further mockery, two thieves with him. So it is written in the Bible.

But the faith of Islam came with views quite different from that of the extend gospels with regards to both the end of Jesus and his nature.

The Glorious Qur'an affirms that Allah the Exalted did not permit the people of Israel to kill Jesus or crucify him. What happened was that Allah saved him from his enemies and raised him to heaven. They never killed Jesus, they killed someone else.

Allah the Almighty declared: *And because of their saying (in boast), "We killed Messiah Jesus, son of Mary, the Messenger of Allah," but they killed him not, nor crucified him, but the resemblance of Jesus was put over another man (and they killed that man) and those who differ therein are full of doubts. They have no certain knowledge, they follow nothing but conjecture. For surely; they killed him not (Jesus, son of Mary): But Allah raised him (Jesus) up (with his body and soul) unto Himself (and he is in the heavens). And Allah is Ever All Powerful, All Wise.*

And there is none of the people of the Scripture (Jews & Christians), but must believe in him (Jesus, son of Mary, as only a Messenger of Allah, and a human being0, before his (Jesus or a Jew's or a Christian's) death (at the time of the appearance of the angel of death). And on the Day of Resurrection, he (Jesus) will be a witness against them. (Ch 4:157-159 Quran)

Almighty Allah also revealed: And remember when Allah said: "O Jesus! I will take you and raise you to Myself and clear you (of the forged statement that Jesus is Allah's son) of those who disbelieve, and I will make those who follow you (Monotheists, who worship none but Allah) superior to those who disbelieve (in the Oneness of Allah, or disbelieve in some of His Messengers, e.g. Muhammad, Jesus, Moses, etc., or in His Holy Books, e.g. the Torah, the Gospel, the Qur'an) till the Day of Resurrection. Then you will return to Me and I will judge between you in the matters in which you used to dispute." (Ch 3:55 Quran).

<hr>

Almighty Allah refuted the claims of the Jews and the Christians in many verses of the Glorious *Qur'a*n.

And hey say: "The Most Beneficent (Allah) has begotten a son (or offspring or children) (as the Jews say: Ezra is the son of Allah, and the Christians say that He has begotten a son (Christ), and the pagan Arabs say that he has begotten daughters (angels, etc.))."

Indeed you have brought forth (said) a terrible evil thing. Whereby the heavens are almost torn, and the earth is split asunder, and the mountains fall in ruins, that they ascribe a son (or offspring or children) to the Most Beneficent (Allah).

But it is not suitable for (the Majesty of) the Most Beneficent (Allah) that He should beget a son (or offspring or children). There is non in the heavens and the earth but comes unto the Most Beneficent (Allah) as a slave. Verily, He knows each one of them, and has counted them a full counting. And everyone of them will come to Him alone on the Day of Resurrection (without any helper, or protector or defender). (Ch 19:88-95 Quran)

Allah the Exalted also declared: Yet, they join the jinns as partners in worship with Allah, though He has created them (the jinns), and they attribute falsely without knowledge sons and daughters to Him. Be He Glorified! And Exalted above (all) that they attribute to Him. He is the Originator of the heavens and the earth. How can He have children when He has no wife? He created all things and He is the All-Knower of everything.

Such is Allah, your Lord! La ilaha illa Huwa (none has the right to be worshipped but He), the Creator of all things. So worship Him (Alone), and He is the Wakil (Trustee, Disposer of affairs, Guardian etc.) over all tings.

No vision can grasp Him, but His Grasp is over all vision. He is the Most Subtle and Courteous, Well-Acquainted with all things. (Ch 6:100-103 Quran)

Almighty Allah commanded: O people of the Scripture (Jews and Christians)! Do not exceed the limits in you religion, nor say of Allah aught but the truth. The Messiah Jesus, son of Mary, was (no more than) a Messenger of Allah and His Word, ("Be" - and he was) which He bestowed on Mary and a spirit (Ruh) created by Him; so believe in Allah and His Messengers. Say not: "Three (trinity)!" Cease! (It is) better for you. For Allah is the only One Ilah (God), Glory be to Him (Far Exalted is He) above having a son. To Him belongs all that is in the heavens and all that is in the earth. And Allah is All Sufficient as a Disposer of affairs.

The Messiah will never be proud to reject to be a slave to Allah, nor the angels who are near (to Allah). And whosoever rejects His worship and is proud, then He will gather them all together unto Himself. So, as for those who believed (in the Oneness of Allah - Islamic Monotheism) and did deeds of righteousness, He will give their (due) rewards, and more out of His Bounty. But as for those who refuse His worship and were proud, He will punish them with a painful torment. And they will not find for themselves besides Allah any protector or helper. (Ch 4:171-173 Quran)

Almighty Allah also declared: And the Jews say: Ezra is the son of Allah, and the Christians say: Messiah is the son of Allah. That is a saying from their mouths. They imitate the saying of the disbeliveers of old. Allah's Curse be on them, how they are deluded away from the truth!

They (Jews and Christians) took their rabbis and their monks to be their lords besides Allah, (by obeying them in things which they made lawful or unlawful according to their own desires without being ordered by Allah) and (they also took as their lord) Messiah, son of Mary, while they (Jews and Christians) were commanded (in the Torah and the Gospel) to worship none but One Ilah (God- Allah) La ilaha illa Huwa (none has the right to be worshipped but He). Praise and glory be to Him, (far above is He) from having the partners they associate (with Him). (Ch 9:30-32 Quran)

Allah the Almighty also revealed: Now ask them (O Muhammad): "Are there (only) daughters for your Lord and sons for them?" Or did We create the angels females while they were witnesses?

Verily, it is of their falsehood that they (Quraish pagans) say: "Allah has begotten off-spring or children (angels are the daughters of Allah)" And, verily, they are liars!

Has He (then) chosen daughters rather than sons? What is the matter with you? How do you decide? Will you not then remember? Or is there for you a plain authority? Then bring your Book if you are truthful!

And they have invented a kinship between Him and the jinns, but the jinn know well that they have indeed to appear (before Him) (i.e. they will be brought for accounts).

Glorified be Allah! (He is free) from what they attribute unto Him! Except the slaves of Allah, whom He chooses (for His Mercy i.e. true believers of Islamic Monotheism who do not attribute false things unto Allah). (Ch 37:149-160 Quran)

And Almighty Allah declared: Surely, in disbelief are they who say that Allah is the Messiah, son of Mary. Say (O Muhammad): "Who then has the least power against Allah, if He were destroy the Messiah, son of Mary, his mother, and all those who are on the earth together?" And to Allah belongs the dominion of the heavens and the earth, and all that is between them. He creates what He wills. And Allah is Able to do all things.

And (both) the Jews and Christians say; "We are the children of Allah and His loved ones." Say: "Why then does He punish you for your sins?" Nay, you are but human beings, of those He has created, He forgive whom He wills and He punishes whom He wills. And to Allah belongs the dominion of the heavens and the earth and all that is between them, and to Him is the return of all.

O people of the Scripture (Jews and Christians)! Now has come to you Our Messenger (Muhammad) making (things) clear unto you, after a break in (the series of) Messengers, lest you say: "there came unto us no bringer of glad tidings and no warner." But now has come unto you a bringer of glad tidings and a warner. And Allah is Able to do all things. (Ch 5:17-19 Quran)

Allah the Exalted warned: Surely they have disbelieved who say: "Allah is the Messiah (Jesus), son of Mary." But the Messiah (Jesus) said: "O Children of Israel! Worship Allah, my Lord and your Lord." Verily, whosoever sets up partners in worship with Allah, then Allah has forbidden Paradise for him, and the Fire will be his abode. And for the Zalimun (polytheists, and wrong-doers) there are no helpers.

Surely, disbeliveers are those who said: "Allah is the third of the three (in a Trinity)." But there is no Ilah (god) (none who has the right to be worshipped) but One Ilah (God- Allah). And if they cease not from what they say, verily, a painful torment will befall the disbeliveers among them.

Will they not repent to Allah and ask His Forgiveness? For Allah is Oft-Forgiving, Most Merciful.

Epilog

The Messiah (Jesus), son of Mary, was no more than a Messenger; many were the Messengers that passed away before him. His mother (Mary) was a Siddiqah (she believed in the Words of Allah, and His Books. They both used to eat food, as any other human being, while Allah does not eat). Look how We made the Ayat (proofs, evidences, verses, lessons, signs, revelations, etc.) clear to them, yet look how they are deluded away from the truth. (Ch 5:72-75 Quran)

And Almighty Allah ordered: And say: "All the praises and thanks be to Allah, Who has not begotten a son (nor an offspring), and Who has no partner in His Dominion, nor He is low to have a Wali (helper, protector, or supporter). And magnify Him with all the magnificence, (Allahu-Akbar, Allah is the Most Great)." (Ch 17:111 Quran)

The pagans once asked the Prophet Muhammad (pbuh): "To whom is your Lord related, His original ancestors and His various branches of descendants?" It is also reported that the Jews said: "We worship Ezra, the Son of Allah," and the Christians said: "Jesus is the Son of Allah," and the Magians said: "We worship the sun and the moon," an the Pagans said: "We worship idols."

In response to all of them Allah revealed some of His attributes: Unity, Uniqueness, and other substantives:

Say: (O Muhammad): "He is Allah, the One. Allah As-Samad (The Self- Sufficient Master, Whom all creatures need, He neither eats nor drinks). He begets not, nor was He begotten; and there is none co-equal or comparable unto Him." (Ch 112:1-4 Quran)

Lightning Source UK Ltd.
Milton Keynes UK
UKHW020622181019
351846UK00011B/821/P